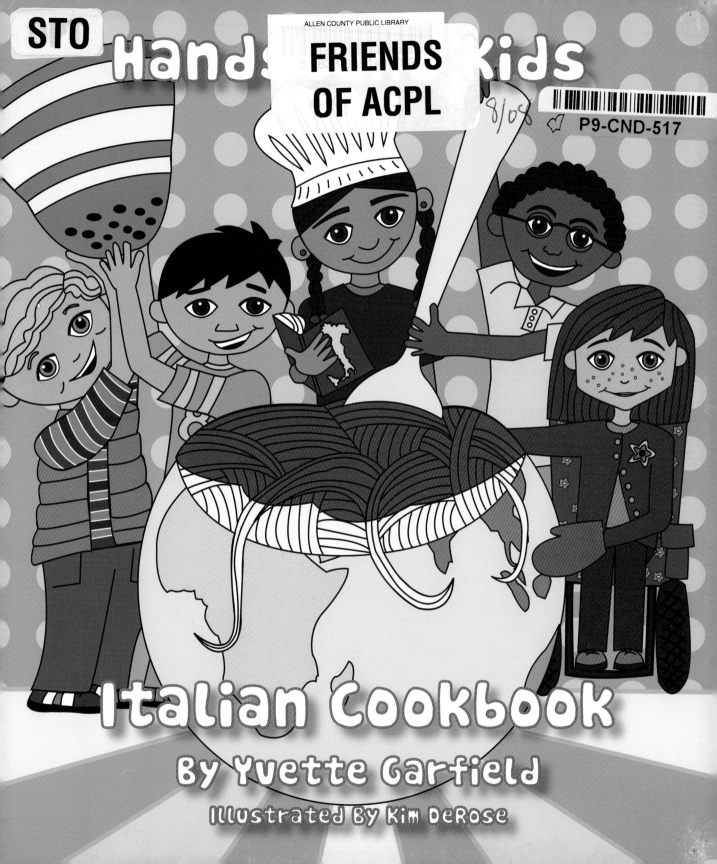

Hands On Kids

Italian Cookbook

By Yvette Garfield

Illustrated By Kim DeRose

Published By Handstand Kids, LLC
Printed In China.
ISBN: 978-0-9792107-0-9

By Yvette Garfield
Illustrated By Kim DeRose
Designed By Vani Sodhi Gundara
Recipe Editing By Liza Yee
Editing By Avital Binshtock

This Book Belongs To:

Dedication

This book is dedicated to my parents who have provided me unconditional love and support in all my ventures. Their enthusiasm for life and exploring the world has inspired me to travel and to pursue my dreams. All my life's successes are because of my mom and dad!

Special Thanks

To my friends whose continued support keeps me going, especially those of you who tasted my recipes as I was learning to be a better cook.

To everyone who worked on the book with me, thank you for helping my dreams come true. Kim DeRose's talent, passion, and creativity continue to impress and inspire me. Liza Yee's recipes always leave me wondering how she makes food taste so good. Vani Gundara's flair for design and dedication to her craft motivates me to work harder. Without the genius of Smriti Mundhra, Brad Sample, and Tracy Sway this book would not have been possible.

Introduction

Welcome to the Handstand Kids cook book series! Food is a fun and hands-on way to learn about other cultures. By learning the recipes of Italy, you are opening your kitchen to a world of experiences. While people around the world have many differences, they all have delicious recipes that are special to their region.

The Handstand Kids (Ari, Felix, Gabby, Izzy, and Marvin) will introduce you to Italian cooking. While making some of Italy's tastiest and most nutritious recipes, you will be introduced to the Italian language. You are on your way to becoming an authentic Italian chef!

After each traditional Italian recipe, there is an alternative suggestion that encourages you to add your own favorite flavors and creativity.

An adult supervisor must be present in the kitchen at all times! The adult supervisor should assist kid chefs when cooking over the stove and using sharp objects. Adult supervision will ensure that kid chefs are always safe in the kitchen.

Cooking is not only fun, but it is a wonderful skill that you can use to help people. Preparing a special meal for a loved one will make anyone's day! Bake sales and food fundraisers are great ways to raise money for a local group. There are also many charities that allow youth volunteers to help those in need. Please check the Handstand Kids website for volunteer opportunities (www.handstandkids.com).

It is my hope that the Handstand Kids cookbook series will provide you with a fun and tasty way to learn about other places and people. I also hope that Handstand Kids books inspire you to make the world a more flavorful place.

So roll up your sleeves, put on your chef's hat, and let the fun begin!

Ciao!
Yvette Garfield

Utensils

Baking Pan

Teglia

Baking Sheet

Placca Da Forno

Blender

Frullatore

Bowls (large, medium, small)

**Piatti Fondi
(grande, medio, piccolo)**

Cupcake Sheet

Teglia Per Pasticcini

Cutting Board

Tagliere

Drinking Glass

Bicchiere

Electric Mixer

Miscelatore

Fork

Forchetta

Grater

Grattugia

Ice Cream Scooper

Cucchiaio Per Gelato

Ice Trays

Portaghiaccio

Knife

Coltello

Large Plate
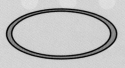
Piatto Grande

Large Pot

Pentolo Grande

in English and Italian:

Measuring Cup

Dosatrice

Measuring Spoon

Cucchiaio Di Misura

Microwave Safe Bowl

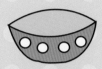

Piatto Fondo Per Microonde

Oven Mitt

Guanto Da Forno

Oven-Safe Dish

Piatto Da Forno

Pastry Brush

Spazzolino Da Cucinare

Rolling Pin

Matterello

Saucepan (medium, small)

Pentola (media, piccola)

Soup Pot

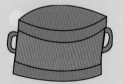

Casseruola

Spatula

Spatola

Spoon

Cucchiaio

Strainer

Passino

Tongs

Pinze

Wooden Spoon

Cucchiaio Di Legno

Ingredients in English and Italian:

Basil	Bread	Eggplant	Eggs	Garlic

Basilico	*Pane*	*Melanzane*	*Uovo (singular), Uova (plural)*	*Aglio*

Fontina	Mozzarella	Parmesan	Ricotta
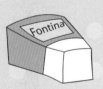			
Fontina	*Mozzarella*	*Parmigiano*	*Ricotta*

Ice Cream	Lemon	Mint	Oil	Onion

Gelato	*Limone*	*Menta*	*Olio*	*Cipolla*

Popcorn	Salt and Pepper	Sugar	Tomatoes

Popcorn	*Sale e Pepe*	*Zucchero*	*Pomodori*

Spaghetti	Macaroni	Tomato Sauce	Pesto Sauce	Butter
				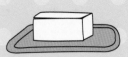
Spaghetti	*Maccheroni*	*Marinara*	*Pesto*	*Burro*

Recipe Levels: Garlic Cloves

Look for the Garlic cloves at the top of the recipe to determine its level of difficulty. Each recipe is ranked from 1 to 4 Garlic cloves — more cloves means that more adult help is encouraged.

Remember, an adult supervisor must be in the kitchen at all times!

1 clove means that this is a Basic recipe and that you can do most of the steps yourself.

2 cloves means that there are some steps that an adult will need to supervise.

3 cloves means that an adult will need to handle certain steps.

4 cloves means that an adult will need to oversee the entire recipe.

Meet The

IZZY

Birthday February 8

Hey! I'm Izzy and I'm 10½ years old. I like spaghetti a lot, but everyone says I am the pickiest eater that they know. If I had it my way, I would eat spaghetti for every meal, even breakfast! But my Grandma says it's better to eat all kinds of foods.

I like making spaghetti, but I am excited to make a dessert that my sister can eat. She is a diabetic so she can't eat food with sugar. I want to make her the Italian ice cream, tartufo, with sugar-free ice cream and we can use toppings (like nuts) that don't have sugar. I think they will taste good, especially after the spaghetti!

FELIX

Birthday July 5

Greetings! I'm Felix and I am 9 years old. I am starting a new school next year and they offer cooking classes after school. I am a vegetarian which means that I don't eat any meat. My whole family is vegetarian so we all love having lasagna for holidays.

I have never cooked anything before and I really want to learn how to make popcorn. I always eat popcorn for a snack at school and of course at the movies. I think it would be really cool to make Italian popcorn at home.

Handstand Kids

GABBY

Birthday October 7

Hi! I'm Gabby and I just turned 11 years old. My favorite thing to do is learn new languages. So far I can speak 3 languages pretty well; English, Spanish, and Farsi. I absolutely love learning new words and I hope that one day I can speak to everyone in the world in their native language. I know that's ambitious, but I am starting young.

I am super-excited to learn Italian words. My favorite food is pizza and I can't wait to make it at home while speaking Italian!

MARVIN

Birthday April 19

Hi! I'm Marvin and I want to be a chef when I grow up. I'm only 10 so I have tons to learn. My mom teaches me a lot of stuff when she's cooking. She has traveled a lot so we make all different kinds of food. When I was 8, she took me to Italy and I loved eating the panini sandwiches. They are so good because they are super-toasty and really easy to make.

I can't wait to have my own restaurant and serve all kinds of panini sandwiches.

ARI

Birthday December 17

Hello there. My name is Ari and I am 8 years old. I love to eat all kinds of foods! My family thinks I am funny because I will try almost any food. One time at a party, I tasted clams. Some of my friends thought they would be slimy and gross, but they were actually really good.

Last Thanksgiving, my family volunteered at a homeless shelter and we gave meals to a lot of families. I know the shelter takes food donations and I am really excited to learn new recipes to bring to them. My favorite food of all time is cookies and I can't wait to make and share biscotti cookies dipped in chocolate. Yum!

Stir It Up!

Congratulations on becoming an Italian chef!

Not only is it fun to make Italian food, but this new skill can help other people. Cooking can help your own community and communities around the world. Bake sales and food fundraisers are wonderful ways to raise money for a local group. There are also many charities that allow youth volunteers to help those in need.

Many wonderful charities and non-profit organizations work very hard to make sure that children around the world are safe and have enough food to eat. You can use your new cooking skills to support these efforts.

Please check the Handstand Kids website for volunteer opportunities. Email us your stories on how your new cooking skills were able to make a difference in someone else's life.

Visit us at: www.handstandkids.com
Contact us at: info@handstandkids.com

Table of Contents

12

13

Contents

The
Oxford Nursery
Treasury

Ian Beck

OXFORD
UNIVERSITY PRESS

For Lily

The Oxford Nursery Treasury

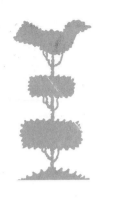

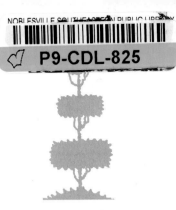

j 398.8 Bec 2000
Beck, Ian.
The Oxford nursery treasury

01/02

All Kids Love ...

14

Foot-Long Garlic Bread

Level

Ingredients

1 loaf of Italian Bread (*pane*)

¼ cup of extra virgin olive oil (*olio*)

3 cloves of garlic (*aglio*), minced

1 cup of grated parmesan cheese (*parmigano*) to sprinkle on top

½ of a lemon

Tools

Cutting Board

Knife

Measuring cups

Microwave-safe bowl

Pastry Brush

Instructions

1. Preheat the toaster oven on the broiler setting.

2. Slice the *pane* in half lengthwise.

3. With the knife, chop the *aglio* into tiny pieces. Put the *olio* and *aglio* into a microwave-safe bowl and cook for 45 seconds.

4. Squeeze the ½ of a *limone* into the heated *olio* and *aglio*. Using the pastry brush, spread this mixture onto each half of the *pane*.

5. Sprinkle the *parmigiano* on top of the bread. Wearing an oven mitt, place the loaf into the oven for about 6 minutes, until the edges have browned.

6. Remove the loaf from the oven and slice each half of the *pane* into 6 pieces.

Alternative

Add sliced tomatoes on top of the toasted garlic bread and eat as a delicious afterschool snack.

16

Mamma's Spaghetti and Meatballs

Level  Serves 4-6

Marinara Sauce Ingredients

A large pot of water
2 pounds (32 ounces) of canned, peeled, and chopped tomatoes (*pomodori*)
3 tablespoons of extra virgin olive oil (*olio*)
1 medium-sized yellow onion, chopped (*cipolla*)
3 cloves of garlic (*aglio*), chopped
1 handful of your favorite vegetables (mushrooms, bell peppers, carrots, celery)
2 teaspoons of sugar
5 leaves of torn basil (*basilica*)
2 teaspoons of salt (*sale*)
1 teaspoon of pepper (*pepe*)

Tools

Cutting Board
Knife
Measuring spoon
Saucepan
Wooden spoon

Instructions

1. Chop the **cipolla** and **aglio** into small pieces. Over a medium heat, pour **olio** into the saucepan and add the **cipolla** and **aglio** for 3 minutes, until onions are soft.

2. Add the chopped **pomodori** and stir in the **zucchero**, **sale** and **pepe**.

3. Turn the heat to low for 30 minutes and add torn **basilica** into the sauce.

Polpette di Carne (Meatballs) Ingredients

1 pound of ground beef or pork
3/4 cup of grated parmesan cheese (*parmigiano*)
2 eggs (*uovo*)
4 cloves of chopped garlic (*aglio*)
2 tablespoons of salt (*sale*)
1 tablespoon of pepper (*pepe*)

Tools

Baking sheet
Large bowl
Measuring cups and spoons

Instructions

1. Preheat the oven to 375 degrees F.

2. Mix all the ingredients in a large bowl using clean hands.

3. Shape the meat into ping-pong sized balls.

4. Place the meatballs on a baking sheet and into the oven for 25 to 30 minutes.

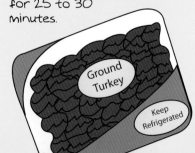

Spaghetti Ingredients

1 pot of water
1 teaspoon of extra virgin olive oil (*olio*)
2 large handfuls of **spaghetti**

Tools

Large pot
Strainer
Tongs
Wooden spoon

Instructions

1. Pour the **olio** into the pot of water and add the spaghetti once it begins to boil.

2. Cook the **spaghetti** for 8 minutes or until the noodles are soft. Wearing oven mitts, carefully pour the pot of **spaghetti** and water into a strainer in the sink.

3. Using tongs, place a serving of spaghetti onto a plate and add the **marinara** and meatballs.

Alternative

For a healthier choice, use ground turkey for the meatballs. For a meatball sandwich, stuff 4 meatballs into a bread roll and add the **marinara** and **parmigiano** on top!

Oh My, Pizza Pie!

Level

Ingredients

Ready-made dough

1 jar (26 ounces) of **marinara** sauce

12 ounces of grated **mozzarella** cheese

Optional toppings (mushrooms, spinach, pepperoni, tomatoes, eggplant, sausage)

½ cup of flour

Tools

Baking sheet
Cutting board
Knife
Rolling pin

Serves 4-5

Instructions

1. Preheat the oven to 400 degrees F.

2. Take the dough out of the refrigerator and let it sit for 30 to 60 minutes.

3. Oil a large baking sheet and stretch the dough into a big circle with the edges a little thicker to hold it better.

4. Sprinkle the dough with flour and use a rolling pin to even out the dough. Continue to add flour as needed so that the dough does not stick to the rolling pin.

5. Spoon a layer of sauce onto the pizza, but leave the edges plain.

6. Sprinkle the **mozzarella** all over the pizza.

7. Add all the toppings that you love!

8. Place the pizza in the oven for 10 to 12 minutes or until the crust is golden brown.

Alternative

Try using **pesto** instead of **marinara** for your pizza sauce to give it a rich flavor and green color.

The Best-O Chicken Pest-O

Level

Serves 4

Pesto Ingredients

4 cups of loosely packed basil *(basilica)*
1½ cups of pine nuts *(pignoli)*
3 or 4 cloves of garlic *(aglio)*
½ cup of parmesan cheese *(parmigiano)*
¾ cup of extra virgin olive oil *(olio)*
1 teaspoon of salt *(sale)*

Tools

Food processor or blender
Measuring cups and spoons

Instructions

Pour all ingredients into the food processor or blender and mix until there is a thick, green paste.

Chicken Ingredients

4 chicken breasts
4 tablespoons of **pesto** sauce
2 teaspoons of olive oil *(olio)*

Tools

Baking sheet
Cutting board
Knife
Measuring spoons
Oven mitts
Pastry brush

Instructions

1. Preheat the oven to 375 degrees F.

2. Slice a pocket into the flat side of the chicken and stuff 1 tablespoon of **pesto** sauce into each chicken breast.

3. Place the chicken onto an oiled baking sheet. Use the pastry brush to oil the tops of the chicken.

4. Bake in the oven for 20 minutes and carefully remove the sheet with oven mitts.

Alternative

Try **pesto** on everything! Vegetarians will love **pesto** on baked eggplant slices. Also, try spreading **pesto** on bread or fresh vegetables.

22

Nutritious
&
Delicious

24

There's Bread in My Salad!
(Panzanella)

Level

Ingredients

1-day-old country bread loaf *(pane)*, crusts removed

2 tomatoes *(pomodori)*

½ of a red onion *(cipolla)*

½ of a cucumber

15 torn basil *(basilica)* leaves

¾ cup of oil *(olio)*

¾ cup of balsamic vinegar

1 tablespoon of salt *(sale)*

1 teaspoon of pepper *(pepe)*

Tools

Cutting board

Knife

Large bowl

Measuring cups

2 wooden spoons

Instructions

1. Slice the crust off of the bread loaf and cut the bread into bite-sized pieces.

2. Put the bread into a large bowl and lightly sprinkle it with water so that it becomes slightly moistened.

3. Chop all the vegetables and add them to the bowl.

4. Pour the *olio*, vinegar, and *sale* into the bowl and mix everything together with the 2 wooden spoons.

5. Leave the salad in the refrigerator for 30 minutes so that the bread absorbs the flavors.

Alternative

Add the salad on top of baked pizza dough. The salad will be the topping!

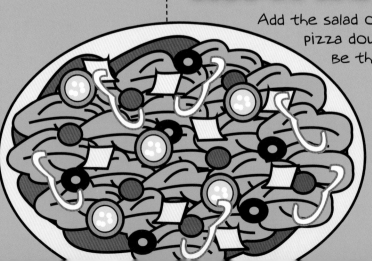

The Leaning Tower of Eggplant

Level

Serves 4

Ingredients

3 medium-sized eggplants *(melanzane)*

2 tablespoons of salt *(sale)*

½ cup of extra virgin olive oil *(olio)*

2 cups of shredded *mozzarella* cheese

Tools

Baking sheet
Cutting board
Knife
Large plate
Measuring cup
2 oven mitts
Paper towels
Pastry brush

Tongs

Alternative

Also try using bell peppers instead of eggplant to make towers of different colors. Try dipping the towers in marinara.

Instructions

1. Preheat the oven to 375 degrees F.

2. Slice *melanzane* into ¼-inch circles.

3. Lay a paper towel onto a plate and sprinkle on a few shakes of *sale*.

4. Place a layer of *melanzane* rounds on top of the paper towel and sprinkle *sale* on top of the *melanzane* rounds before covering them with another paper towel.

5. Sprinkle that paper towel with *sale* and stack more *melanzane* rounds until it is completely laid out.

6. Allow the *melanzane* to "sweat" for 20 minutes so that the moisture is absorbed into the paper towels.

7. Oil the baking pan and place *melanzane* slices onto the pan.

8. Using the pastry brush, apply the *olio* on the tops of the *melanzane* and leave them in the oven for 15 minutes.

9. Wearing oven mitts, remove the baking sheet from the oven. With tongs, place the *melanzane* slices onto the large plate and sprinkle on the *mozzarella*.

10. When the *melanzane* has cooled, stack them to form a leaning tower.

28

Mamma Mia Minestrone
(Vegetable Soup)

Level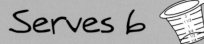

Serves 6

Ingredients

1 can (15 ounces) of red beans

1 can (12 ounces) of whole peeled tomatoes *(pomodori)*

1 yellow onion *(cipolla)*

½ cup of parmesan, grated *(parmigiano)*

2 potatoes

2 cups of green beans

2 chopped tomatoes *(pomodori)*

2 cups of zucchini

2 cups of mushrooms

2 cups of celery

1 quart of vegetable or chicken broth

3 quarts of water

Salt and pepper *(sale e pepe)*

2 cups of macaroni *(maccheroni)*

Tools

Cutting board

Knife

Large pot

Measuring cups

2 oven mitts

Wooden spoon

Instructions

1. Chop the vegetables and potatoes into bite-sized pieces.

2. Place all the ingredients, except the *maccheroni* and *parmigiano*, into the large pot on the stove on a high heat setting.

3. When the water boils, pour in the *maccheroni* while wearing oven mitts and let it cook for 30 minutes on medium heat.

4. Spoon the soup into bowls and sprinkle with *parmigiano*.

Alternative

For a heartier soup, add a handful of cooked meatballs into the pot 5 minutes before the soup is ready.

30

Mangia La Lasagna

Level

Ingredients

1 package of no-boil or fresh lasagna noodles

2 pounds of *marinara* or meat sauce

8 ounces of spinach

15 ounces of *ricotta* cheese

1 pound of grated *mozzarella* cheese

½ cup of parmesan cheese *(parmigiano)*

Tools

Aluminum foil
Large bowl
Oven-safe dish
Wooden spoon

Alternative

Add 2 tablespoons of *pesto* to the *ricotta* layer for a rich flavor!

Serves 6-8

Instructions

1. Preheat the oven to 400 degrees F.

2. Using the wooden spoon, mix the *ricotta* with the spinach in the large bowl.

3. Pour a thin layer of *marinara* on the bottom of the oven-safe dish, just enough to cover the dish.

4. Place a single layer of *lasagna* noodles over the sauce.

5. Put a layer of the *ricotta* mixture on top of the noodles and use your hands to make even layers.

6. Sprinkle a layer of *mozzarella* on top.

7. Pour on another layer of *marinara* sauce.

8. Repeat steps 4 through 7.

9. Put another layer of noodles on top and sprinkle on the rest of the *mozzarella* and *parmigiano*.

10. Pour a thin layer of *marinara* sauce to completely cover the top layer.

11. Cover the dish with aluminum foil and bake in the oven for 35 minutes.

12. Remove the foil and bake for another 5 to 10 minutes, until the cheese is slightly browned.

13. Allow the *lasagna* to cool for about 10 minutes before serving.

Italianize My ....

Sparkling Water into Italian Soda

Level

Serves 3

Ingredients

24 ounces of sparkling water

6 tablespoons of flavored syrup (raspberry, strawberry, or another yummy flavor)

2 cups of water

A few springs of mint (*menta*)

Tools

Measuring cup
2 ice trays
Stirring spoon
3 tall drinking glasses

Instructions

1. Pour 8 ounces of the sparkling water into each glass.

2. Add 2 tablespoons of your choice of flavored syrup into each glass.

3. Use a long spoon to mix the syrup and water together.

Sparkling Water

Alternative

The night before making Italian soda, add small sprigs of *menta* to the ice tray. Your Italian soda will look beautiful with a great *menta* flavor!

Popcorn into Italian Popcorn

Level

Serves 2

Ingredients

1 bag of plain microwave popcorn or ½ cup of popcorn kernels

1 tablespoon of olive oil **(olio)**

¼ cup of grated parmesan **(parmigiano)**, grated

1 teaspoon of dried oregano

½ teaspoon of paprika

Tools

2 brown lunch bags
1 large bowl
2 oven mitts
2 wooden spoons

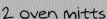

Instructions

1. Mix the **olio**, **parmigiano**, oregano, and paprika in the bowl.

2. Pop the popcorn in the microwave or pop the kernels in a popcorn machine.

3. Wearing oven mitts, divide the popped kernels into the 2 lunch bags.

4. Evenly pour the flavor mixture over the popcorn and shake the bag for 30 seconds.

5. Enjoy!

Alternative

To add a little spice, sprinkle on red chili flakes instead of the paprika. Start with a very tiny pinch of chili to make sure it is not too spicy.

Sandwiches into Panini

Level

Ingredients

3 Italian bread rolls (*pane*)

Mozzarella, parmesan (*parmigiano*), or *fontina* cheese

Sliced deli meat (turkey, roast beef, or pastrami)

½ cup of extra virgin olive oil (*olio*)

Tools

Cutting board
Knife
2 oven mitts
1 pastry brush
2 saucepans (1 medium and 1 small)
Tongs

Alternative

Make vegetarian *panini* by filling the bread with sliced tomatoes, *mozzarella*, basil, and eggplant!

Serves 2-3

Instructions

1. Slice the *pane* in half and open the roll, placing the meat and cheese inside. Use the pastry brush to apply the *olio* to the top and bottom of the *pane* roll.

2. Heat both the small and medium-sized saucepans on a medium fire and pour about 1 tablespoon of *olio* into the medium-sized saucepan.

3. Wearing oven mitts, place the sandwich in the medium-sized saucepan. Place the bottom of the smaller pan on the top of the roll to heat the *pane* and squish it down.

4. Keep the smaller pan on the sandwich for 2 minutes and then use the tongs to turn the sandwich over. Reapply the small saucepan to the roll for 2 minutes.

5. Using the tongs, place the *panini* onto a plate.

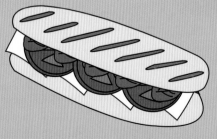

Mac and Cheese into Maccheroni e Formaggio

Level  🧄 🧄 🧄   Serves 4

Ingredients

12 ounces of macaroni
(**maccheroni**) pasta

3/4 cup of milk (lowfat or
regular)

2½ cups of shredded **mozzarella**
cheese

2 cups of chopped
vegetables (spinach,
broccoli, or any other
favorites)

10 cups of water

Tools

Large pot
Measuring cups
2 oven mitts
Strainer
Wooden spoon

Instructions

1. Boil 10 cups of water in the large pot,
enough to completely cover the pasta.

2. Wearing the oven mitts, add the
maccheroni to the pot and cook for
7 to 9 minutes.

3. Drain the pasta into a
strainer in the
sink. Pour the
maccheroni back
into the pot
and stir in the milk and
mozzarella until they are
evenly distributed.

4. Add the vegetables to the
pot and stir well for 3 to
5 minutes. Use the wooden spoon to
scoop the **maccheroni** into a serving
bowl.

Alternative

Add bite-sized pieces of protein
(cooked chicken, beef, or tofu)
to the pasta to make it a complete
meal.

42

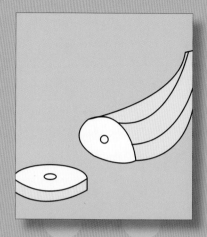

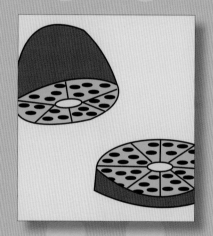

sugar

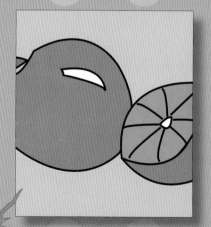

Lemon Juice

gelato

Save Room For ....

44

Bella Biscotti Cookies

Level  Makes about 20 biscotti cookies

Ingredients

2½ cups of flour

¾ teaspoon of salt *(sale)*

2 teaspoons of baking powder

1¼ cups of sugar *(zucchero)*, plus more for sprinkling

5 eggs *(uovo)*

1 teaspoon of vanilla extract

1 cup of toasted whole almonds

1 teaspoon of cinnamon

1 tablespoon of butter *(burro)*

Tools

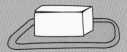

Baking sheet
Cutting board
Large bowl
Measuring cups and spoons
Serrated knife
Small bowl
Wooden spoon

Alternative

Add 1 cup of chocolate chips to the dough. Also, melt chocolate chips in the microwave for 1 minute and dip the ends of the cooled *biscotti* into the mixture. Refrigerate for 1 hour.

Instructions

1. Preheat the oven to 375 degrees F.

2. Grease the large baking sheet with a light coat of *burro* and then sprinkle the sheet with flour.

3. Mix the flour, *zucchero*, baking powder, and *sale* together in the large bowl and make a hole in the middle of the mixture.

4. Add the 4 *uovo*, cinnamon, and vanilla into the hole and use the wooden spoon to stir thoroughly.

5. Mix the almonds evenly throughout the dough. Then, using your hands, shape the dough into 2 logs.

6. Place each log onto the baking sheet, leaving 4 inches between the edges of the sheet and the dough.

7. Beat 1 *uovo* in the small bowl and use the pastry brush to coat the *uovo* on the logs.

8. Bake the logs in the oven for 15 minutes, until they are a nice golden-brown color.

9. Allow the logs to cool for 10 minutes. Place them on the cutting board and cut them diagonally into 2-inch slices.

10. Arrange the slices back onto the baking sheet so that the cut sides are facing up. Bake for another 5 minutes.

11. Cool the slices and bite into the crunchy goodness!

Grandisimo Granita Ices

Level

Serves 4

Ingredients

3 lemons *(limone)*

½ cup of sugar *(zucchero)*

2 cups cold water

Tools

Medium-sized bowl

Fork

Grater

Measuring cups

Plastic wrap

Saucepan

Shallow, freezable container

Wooden spoon

Alternative

Try using different fruits each time you make *granita* to find your very favorite flavor. Watermelon is great too!

Instructions

1. Grate the *limone* rind and then squeeze the juice of the 3 *limone* into the bowl.

2. Place the *limone* juice, *zucchero*, and *limone* rinds in a saucepan and bring the mixture to a boil.

3. Turn the heat to low for about 5 minutes until a thick, syrupy liquid forms.

4. Cool the mixture to room temperature and mix in the 2 cups of cold water.

5. Pour the mixture into a shallow container and then cover it with a lid or cling wrap.

6. Freeze the *granita* for about an hour and then use a fork to break it up. Put it back into the freezer and repeat 3 times, every hour, for 3 hours.

7. Scoop the *granita* out of the container and enjoy!

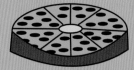

48

Torta al Cioccolato

Level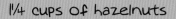

Serves 8

Ingredients

1¼ cups of hazelnuts

¼ cup of all-purpose flour

1 teaspoon of cinnamon

8 ounces of semisweet chocolate chips

1 stick of butter *(burro)*

1 cup of sugar *(zucchero)*

7 eggs *(uovo)*

Powdered sugar

Tools

Baking pan
Electric mixer
Food processor
1 large bowl
Measuring cups
3 medium-sized bowls
Microwave-safe bowl
2 oven mitts
Spatula
Toothpicks
Wax paper

Alternative

Pour the batter into cupcake tins to make individual *torta*. The cupcakes will only need to bake for 15 minutes.

Instructions

1. Preheat the oven to 350 degrees F.

2. Line the bottom of a baking pan with waxed paper and then apply the *burro* to the pan.

3. Grind the nuts and flour together in the food processor until they have the consistency of fine sand.

4. Pour the chocolate chips in the microwave-safe bowl and microwave them for 2 minutes. Wear oven mitts when removing the bowl.

5. Use the electric mixer to beat the *burro* with a ½ cup of *zucchero* until it is fluffy.

6. Stir the chocolate and beat it into the *burro* mixture.

7. Separate the *uovo* yolks and whites into different bowls.

8. Slowly beat the *uovo* yolks into the *burro-zucchero* blend. Continue to beat the mixture for 2 minutes after the last yolk has been added. Then stir in the hazelnut-flour mixture..

9. In a clean, dry bowl, beat the *uovo* whites with the electric mixer and add ½ cup of *zucchero.* Beat until the uovo whites stand up when the mixer is removed.

10. Fold the *uovo* whites into the chocolate batter using the spatula.

11. Pour the batter into the pan and place it into the oven for 40 to 45 minutes.

12. Once the *torta* has cooled, sprinkle powdered sugar on top of it.

Every Tummy Loves Tartufo
(Chocolate-Dipped Ice Cream)

Level 🧄

Ingredients

10 chocolate cookies

1 pint of ice cream *(gelato)*

8 ounces of chocolate chips

1 tablespoon of vegetable oil *(olio)*

Tools

Aluminum foil

Baking sheet

Cutting board

Ice cream scooper

Knife

Measuring spoon

Microwave-safe bowl

Alternative

Try adding toppings like chocolate chips or frozen berries to the ice cream before rolling it in the cookies.

Instructions

1. Line the baking sheet with aluminum foil and place it in the freezer.

2. On the cutting board, carefully chop the cookies into bite-sized pieces.

3. Scoop the **gelato** into 6 balls and then roll them into the ground cookie mixture. Place them on the cookie sheet.

4. Freeze the ice cream balls for an hour.

5. Pour the chocolate chips and the **olio** into the bowl and microwave for 2½ minutes.

6. Pour the melted chocolate mixture over the **gelato** balls to lightly coat them. Put them back in the freezer until the chocolate solidifies.

7. In about 30 minutes, the **tartufo** is ready to enjoy!

The Princess and the Pea

O nce upon a time, in a faraway kingdom, there lived a prince. He was an only child, and spoilt a little by his parents. For his twentieth birthday he was given a fine white stallion, called Blaze. One day his father sent for the prince. 'My boy,' he said, 'it is time you set out and found yourself a real princess to marry.' So the prince travelled the length and breadth of the world on Blaze. They rode through summer sun and winter snow. They rode under all the phases of the moon, through deserts and over mountains.

The prince met many girls who said that they were princesses. Girls who curtsied very nicely. Girls with eyes hidden behind painted fans. Girls who danced elegantly in bright, silk dresses. But the prince was never sure if any of them was a real princess. The king and queen had insisted, 'She must be a real princess.' But after all his travels, the prince had never been sure whether any of the girls he had met had been a real princess.

And so, one night, under a new moon, the prince rode back into the palace yard, with his head bowed and a heavy heart. His mother welcomed him back with his favourite meal. 'Come on,' she said, 'sausages, onion gravy, and mashed potatoes. I cooked them myself, this ought to cheer you up.'

But although the prince made a hearty supper, he was still sad. 'I've looked over the whole world, from one end to the other. I'll never find a real princess,' and he sighed.

'Don't worry,' said the queen, 'there are ways of telling a real princess. When the right girl comes, I will find out for you, never fear.'

Summer turned to autumn, and great storms shook the kingdom. Hailstones the size of goose eggs crashed around the palace turrets. A great wind tore up the ancient oak that the prince had played in since his childhood. Then winter came, howling in on a blizzard, and the palace was surrounded with deep drifts of snow; even Blaze was kept in the stable under fleecy blankets.

Then one night, the coldest of the year so far, when even the powdered snow had frozen into hard ice, there was a knocking at the palace door. The king was roused from his warm fireside. 'Who on earth can that be out in this awful weather, and at this late hour?' He set off, wrapped in his warmest cloak, and opened the heavy door.

A girl stood knee deep in a drift of snow. Her fine cape, reduced to rags, was wrapped around her shoulders, and she was huddled and shivering. Her hair was wet around her face, and there were little icicles on her sooty eyelashes. She fell into the king's arms, and he carried her into the warm parlour.

After a few minutes the girl was warmed through. She sat by the fire, drinking a cup of hot chocolate. Some colour had come back into her cheeks, and as she brushed the strands of damp hair away from her face, the prince could see that she might just be beautiful.

The queen stole a glance at her son, and noticed that he was a little smitten with the mysterious girl. 'Tell us about yourself, my dear,' said the queen.

'I am Princess Phoebe,' said the girl. 'I have been travelling the world, seeking a suitable prince to marry.' She shook her head sadly. 'I had searched for nearly a year with no luck, for you see he must be a real prince. I was just on my way home when the blizzard struck. I stabled my poor horse, and then followed the lights here.'

The prince was about to speak out when the queen gestured to him to be quiet. Then she said brightly, 'Well, my dear, you must be exhausted. You must have a hot bath, then we will put you to bed, and in the morning all shall be well.'

While Phoebe was in her bath, the queen took the prince and two servants to the guest bedchamber. She ordered the servants to strip all the bedding from the bed, and start over again. When the mattress was removed the queen took a little silver box from her purse, opened the box, and inside was a single green pea.

The queen took the pea and placed it in the middle of the bed base. Then she ordered the servants to bring as many mattresses and feather quilts as could be found. She had all the mattresses piled one on top of the other, along with all the quilts and covers. When they had finished there must have been fifty or more, reaching almost to the ceiling, and it was a very tall room.

'Now we shall see if she is a real princess,' said the queen. 'Trust me.'

Princess Phoebe spent an uncomfortable night. Despite the duvets, feather mattresses, and cosy warmth, things weren't right. No matter how she lay in the bed, no matter how she twisted and turned, this way and that, it was no good, she couldn't settle, and through all that night she didn't sleep a wink.

In the morning, all looked beautiful in the bright sun-shine. This would be a fine place to live, Phoebe thought, looking across the snow-covered kingdom from the high window. She went down to the parlour for breakfast.

'Good morning, my dear,' said the queen. 'I hope you slept well.'

Phoebe looked tired, and her eyes had dark circles round them. 'I have never spent a more uncomfortable night,' she said. 'I couldn't sleep at all. No matter how I lay in the bed it felt as if something was digging into me.

I must be covered in bruises.'

It was then that the prince understood what his mother had been doing. If this girl had felt such a tiny thing as a pea through all those layers of quilts and feathers, then she must be a real princess.

'Look around you, my dear,' said the queen. 'You will see that this is no ordinary house, it is a palace.'

Phoebe looked at all the silverware on the breakfast table; the fine damasks and silks at the tall windows. At that moment the king entered, dressed in his state robes and accompanied by his lord chamberlain, who carried a crown on a velvet cushion.

'If this is a palace,' said Phoebe, 'then you must be the queen, and there, if I am not mistaken, is the king.' At that she curtsied, and then bounced up with a smile on her face. 'Which means that your son is a real prince.'

Later that day the princess's horse was brought from the stables, a fine black mare with a long silky tail. Together the prince and princess set off to ride in the bright winter sunshine. There was even a promise of spring in the air. 'Mark my words,' said the queen, 'we'd best set the lord chamberlain to preparing the cathedral for a royal wedding.'

And so they did, and later that year the real prince and the real princess were married, and went to live in their own palace by a lake with a good stable for both their fine horses. Soon they had to add a nursery, and so they all lived happily to the end of their days, which was as long a time as it could be.

Jack a Nory

I'll tell you a story
  About Jack a Nory,
And now my story's begun;
I'll tell you another
  Of Jack and his brother,
And now my story is done.

Ride a Cock-Horse

Ride a cock-horse to Banbury Cross,
To see a fine lady upon a white horse;
Rings on her fingers and bells on her toes,
And she shall have music wherever she goes.

Pease Porridge Hot

Pease porridge hot,
Pease porridge cold,
Pease porridge in the pot
Nine days old.
Some like it hot,
Some like it cold,
Some like it in the pot
Nine days old.

Apple Pie

Apple-pie, apple-pie,
Peter likes apple-pie;
So do I, so do I.

Roses are Red

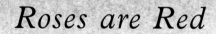

Roses are red,
    Violets are blue,
Sugar is sweet
    And so are you.

Lilies are White

Lilies are white,
    Rosemary's green,
When I am king,
    You shall be queen.

The Tortoise and the Hare

Once upon a time, and as long ago as anyone can remember, there lived a tortoise. His was a slow, steady, and pleasant life. Every winter, while the world was cold and harsh, he would fill up on sweet lettuce and carrots, and then fall fast asleep in his cosy home, until the spring.

Just near the tortoise lived an excitable and bouncy hare. He rushed everywhere at great speed, especially in the spring, when he seemed to be full of extra energy.

So it was one spring morning, when the hare rushed past his neighbour the tortoise on the road. The tortoise had been ambling along, minding his own business. He had only just woken up from his long winter sleep, and was just getting used to the world again, when he was nearly knocked over by the dashing hare.

'Hey, watch where you are going,' said the tortoise. 'We can't all rush about like you.'

'My word,' said the hare, 'but you are a slowcoach.'

Now the tortoise was cross at having been nearly knocked over, and he answered quite snappily, 'Not as slow as you seem to think. Why, I could beat you in a race any day.'

'Oh, really,' said the hare with a laugh. 'I wouldn't bet on it if I were you.'

Just then a fox strolled past, and the hare said, 'This tortoise says he can beat me in a race,' and they both laughed, so that the tortoise got even crosser.

He said, 'I bet you my snug winter den that I can beat you over any distance.'

'I'll bet you a lifetime supply of sweet lettuce and carrots that you can't,' said the hare.

Then the fox said, 'You shall run a race, and I shall judge the winner.'

'Agreed,' said the tortoise and the hare together, and the hare added, 'Easiest bet I've ever won,' and laughed again. The tortoise said nothing, just smiled and shook his head.

So it was that the fox set up a course across the countryside with a start and finish line, and on a bright morning the tortoise and the hare lined up ready to start.

The fox raised his flag, and said, 'Ready,' and the hare raised himself up on his strong back legs, while the tortoise just stood and waited. Then the fox said, 'Steady,' and the hare breathed heavily and puffed out his cheeks, running on the spot, while the tortoise just stood and waited. Then the fox said 'Go!' and dropped the flag, and the hare sprinted away as fast as he could, while the tortoise just ambled forward in a slow and steady way.

The hare ran fast for a while. Then he slowed a little and looked back down the road. There was no sign of the tortoise, he had been left far behind. The hare laughed to himself and stopped altogether. It was a warm morning, and running so fast was tiring work. The hare spotted a nice patch of shade under a tree, and he went and sat there to wait for the tortoise.

31

'It'll be a long wait,' he said, and yawned and stretched. 'I'll just have a little nap.' So the hare settled under the tree and soon fell fast asleep.

The tortoise meanwhile was walking along, not fast, but sure and steady. As it was so warm, and he was hot inside his shell, he stopped and had a nibble of some cooling dandelion leaves, and a drink from a stream. The sun rose higher and hotter, and he ambled on, slow but sure. After what seemed a very long time he drew level with, and then just overtook, a snail. 'Morning, Mr Snail,' said the tortoise.

'Morning, Mr Tortoise,' said the snail. 'If you look over there you can see the hare asleep under that tree.'

'Why, so he is,' said the tortoise, and he shook his head and carried on, and on, down the dusty road.

The hare woke from his refreshing nap. He felt fine, if a little stiff. He stretched and ran up and down for a bit, to ease himself in for the run. Then he climbed the tree and looked back down the road. There was no sign of the tortoise but he could just see a snail, far away on the road. He turned round and he could see the road going the other way, and far off he could see the finish line with the bright banner, and a crowd of animals waiting. He was about to jump down and do some push-ups before setting off again, when he saw something on the road that caused him to fall down from the tree in shock. It was the tortoise plodding along, only yards from the finish line.

The hare picked himself up, and set off again as fast as he could. He crested the hill at great speed, and there, some way ahead of him, was the tortoise, making steady progress, and now only a few feet from the finish line. The hare made a great effort and charged down the final straight. He crossed the line and fell out of breath to the ground. He was too late. The tortoise had crossed the line long before the hare, and was being congratulated by the fox.

'That's a lifetime of sweet lettuce and carrots that the hare owes me,' said the tortoise, with a big smile. 'You see, hare, slow and steady does it.'

And the tortoise lived for a very, very, very long time (as tortoises do) and for all of that time the hare had to make sure he had lots and lots of sweet lettuce and carrots. Except during the long cold winter, of course, when the tortoise was snug and asleep in his burrow, and the hare had all that long, cold time to himself.

Dickery, Dickery, Dare

Dickery, dickery, dare,
The pig flew up in the air;
The man in brown
Soon brought him down,
Dickery, dickery, dare.

See-Saw, Margery Daw

See-saw, Margery Daw,
Jacky shall have a new master;
Jacky shall have but a penny a day,
Because he can't work any faster.

See-saw, Margery Daw,
The old hen flew over the malt house;
She counted her chickens one by one,
Still she missed the little white one,
And this is it, this is it, this is it.

Little Poll Parrot

Little Poll Parrot
Sat in his garret
Eating toast and tea;
A little brown mouse
Jumped into the house,
And stole it all away.

Hoddley, Poddley

Hoddley, poddley, puddle and fogs,
Cats are to marry the poodle dogs;
Cats in blue jackets and dogs in red hats,
What will become of the mice and the rats?

Sing a Song of Sixpence

Sing a song of sixpence,
    A pocket full of rye;
Four and twenty blackbirds,
    Baked in a pie.

When the pie was opened,
    The birds began to sing;
Was not that a dainty dish,
    To set before the king?

The king was in his counting-house,
  Counting out his money;
The queen was in the parlour,
  Eating bread and honey.

The maid was in the garden,
  Hanging out the clothes,
When down came a blackbird
  And pecked off her nose.

Diddlety, Diddlety, Dumpty

Diddlety, diddlety, dumpty,
The cat ran up the plum tree;
Half a crown to fetch her down,
Diddlety, diddlety, dumpty.

42

There Was an Old Crow

There was an old crow
　　Sat upon a clod;
That's the end of my song.
　　—That's odd.

The Porridge Pot

Once upon a time, when the world was a place of forests and magic, there lived a little girl called Ragamuffin. She lived with her mother, in a tiny wooden house, in a tiny village on the edge of a great dark forest. Her mother was very poor, and did the best she could to feed and clothe herself and her little daughter.

However, as autumn ended, and the cold and darkness of winter approached, things went from bad to worse. At last the larder was bare, and there was nothing left for them to eat.

'Don't worry, mother,' said kind little Ragamuffin. 'There may be a few berries left in among the trees. I'll see if I can find some.' And so Ragamuffin set out with her basket on her arm. She walked among the tall trees. It was damp and misty, and gradually Ragamuffin found herself walking deeper and deeper along the twisty paths. She found no berries, no mushrooms, no nuts, nothing.

It was a cold morning, and she shivered and drew her thin cloak around her little shoulders. It was just then that she heard something. A twig cracked and some leaves rustled under the trees. Ragamuffin was frightened. She had heard of the fierce wolves that sometimes prowled about in the deep forest.

But then she heard a friendly voice. 'Is that you, my little Ragamuffin?' And an old lady appeared, leaning on a stout walking stick. She stepped forward from the mist under the trees. 'I know you, little Ragamuffin,' she said.

'You are a good and kind little girl, and helpful to your poor mother, and I know you are both very, very hungry.' The old lady held out a little iron cooking pot. 'Here,' she said, 'take this home with you. It's a very special pot. You must just say to it "Cook, little pot", and it will be filled with lovely nourishing porridge. And when you have both eaten your fill you must remember to say "Enough, little pot", and then the pot will stop making the porridge.'

Ragamuffin took the pot and thanked the old lady. Then she ran back home to her mother as fast as she could, clutching the little pot under her cloak.

When she arrived back at the little house, her mother was sitting at the table, her head sunk in despair. Ragamuffin set the little pot on the bare wooden table. 'Cook, little pot,' she said. At once the kitchen filled with the smell of fresh, warm porridge. Her mother looked up. There was a friendly bubbly sound, and the little pot filled to the brim with what looked like steaming porridge. It was the most delicious porridge they had ever tasted, just sweet enough, and tasting as though it were made with cream fresh from the cow. They ate and ate until they could eat no more. Ragamuffin said, 'Enough, little pot,' and the pot was empty again.

For most of that long, cold winter, Ragamuffin and her mother ate together from the little pot. The porridge stayed as fresh and delicious as ever. Then, one day, Ragamuffin's mother was alone in the house. She thought it could do no harm to have some of the delicious porridge on her own. She fetched the little pot down from its special shelf, and set it down on the table.

She waited for a moment in anticipation, and then said, 'Cook, little pot.' There came the familiar delicious smell, then the little bubbly noise, and then the pot was full, and the mother ate her fill, and then a little more, and then even some more, so that her tummy was nicely warm and rounded. Then the mother closed her eyes in contentment, and fell fast asleep.

She woke up a little later, with the feeling that her chair was afloat on a warm sea. She opened her eyes, and let out a cry. 'OH NO!' The little pot was still bubbling over with porridge. The porridge was pouring over the edge of the pot, it was running all over the table, down the legs, and had filled all the floor of the little house up to the window.

Her chair was floating on a sea of porridge. She held on to the edge of the table and called out to Ragamuffin. You see, she had forgotten the words that would stop the little pot.

She did her best. She called out, 'Do stop all this,' and 'No more porridge,' and, 'That's enough,' but it was no good. More and more porridge kept bubbling out of the pot. It poured through the windows and under the door, it swept through the streets of the little village like a great wave. It swept up under the doors and through the windows of the other villagers, and gradually all the village houses filled up with porridge. One by one the people struggled out through their front doors or windows. Their clothes were covered in the sticky porridge, but goodness it did taste delicious.

At that moment Ragamuffin came home. She shook her head as she stepped through the river of porridge; she had to try hard to keep from bursting out laughing. Just then her greedy mother came floating out of the window on her chair. 'Oh, help, Ragamuffin,' she called out. Then Ragamuffin and all the villagers laughed, and Ragamuffin said, 'Enough, little pot,' and the flow of porridge stopped, and her mother's chair came to a slow and sticky halt.

It took the village the rest of the winter to eat their way through all the lovely porridge. But at least nobody went hungry that year.

A Man in the Wilderness

A man in the wilderness asked me,
How many strawberries grow in the sea.
I answered him, as I thought good,
As many red herrings as swim in the wood.

Tweedledum and Tweedledee

Tweedledum and Tweedledee
   Agreed to have a battle,
For Tweedledum said Tweedledee
   Had spoiled his nice new rattle.
Just then flew by a monstrous crow
   As big as a tar-barrel,
Which frightened both the heroes so,
   They quite forgot their quarrel.

If All the World Was Paper

If all the world was paper,
　And all the sea was ink,
If all the trees were bread and cheese,
　What should we have to drink?

Pretty Maid, Pretty Maid

Pretty maid, pretty maid,
  Where have you been?
Gathering roses
  To give to the queen.
Pretty maid, pretty maid,
  What gave she you?
She gave me a diamond,
  As big as my shoe.

Mr Punchinello

Oh, mother, I shall be married to Mr Punchinello,
　　To Mr Punch,
　　To Mr Joe,
　　To Mr Nell,
　　To Mr Lo,
　　Mr Punch, Mr Joe,
　　Mr Nell, Mr Lo,
　　To Mr Punchinello.

Sally Go Round the Sun

Sally go round the sun,
Sally go round the moon,
Sally go round the chimney-pots
On a Saturday afternoon.

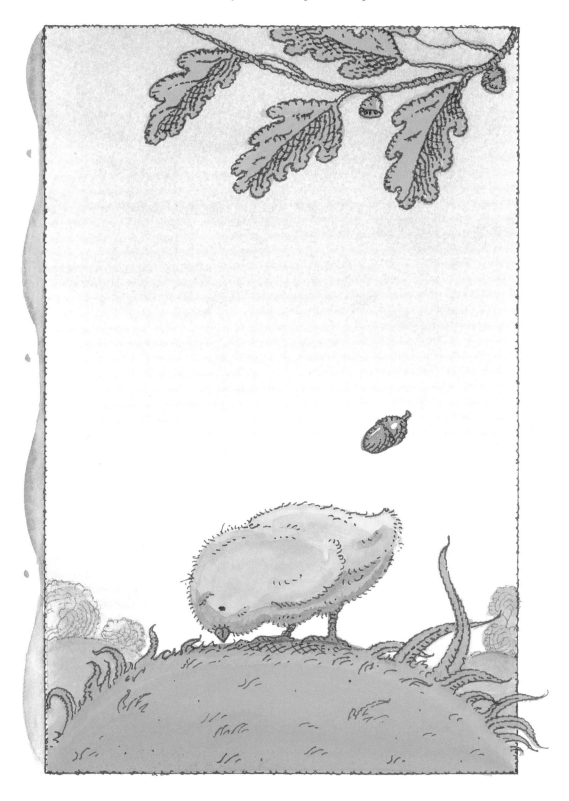

Chicken Licken

Once upon a time, when the world was young and the animals could speak, there was a tiny wee chick called Chicken Licken. Now it happened that fluffy, yellow Chicken Licken was grubbing about in her favourite patch, when an acorn fell, 'plomp', on her little tail. 'Oh no,' said Chicken Licken, 'the sky is falling down. Help, I must go and warn the king.'

So she set off on her busy little feet, and after a while she met her great friend Henny Penny.

'Well well, if it isn't Chicken Licken,' said Henny Penny. 'Where are you off to in such a hurry?'

'Quick, help help, Henny Penny. The sky is falling down, and I must go and warn the king.'

'I see,' said Henny Penny. 'And how can you be so sure that the sky is falling down?'

'Because,' said Chicken Licken, 'I saw it with my own two eyes, heard it with my own two ears, and a piece of the sky landed, plomp, on my own tail.'

'Then I'll come with you,' said Henny Penny.

So they set off together, and tripped along through the grass, until they met Cocky Locky.

'Well, a-doodle well,' said Cocky Locky to Henny Penny and Chicken Licken. 'Where are you two going, may I ask a-doodle do?'

'Oh, help, Cocky Locky. The sky is falling down, and we must go and warn the king.'

'I see,' said Cocky Locky. 'And how do you know the sky is falling a-doodle down?'

'Chicken Licken told me,' said Henny Penny.

'I saw it with my own two eyes, heard it with my own two ears, and a piece of the sky landed, plomp, on my tail,' said Chicken Licken.

'Very well,' said Cocky Locky, 'I will travel with you, and we will warn the king.'

So all three set off skipping through the grass, until they met Ducky Daddles.

'Well, well, well, quack, well,' said Ducky Daddles. 'If it isn't Cocky Locky, Henny Penny, and Chicken Licken. Where are you all off to?'

'Oh, help a-doodle do, the sky is falling down, and we must go and warn the king.'

'But how do you know the sky is falling down?' asked Ducky Daddles.

'Well, Henny Penny told me,' said Cocky Locky.

'Yes, and Chicken Licken told me,' said Henny Penny.

'I saw it with my own two eyes, heard it with my own two ears, and a piece of it landed, plomp, on my own tail,' said Chicken Licken.

'Then I had better, quack, come with you, and we can all warn the king.'

So they set off together, on their brisk little feet, until they met Goosey Loosey.

'A very good morning to you, Ducky Daddles, Cocky Locky, Henny Penny, and Chicken Licken. Where might you all be going in such a rush?'

'Oh, help, Goosey Loosey, the sky is falling down and we must go and warn the king.'

'But how do you know that the sky is falling down?' asked Goosey Loosey, looking up at the bright blue above.

'Cocky Locky told me,' said Ducky Daddles.

'Henny Penny told me,' said Cocky Locky.

'Chicken Licken told me,' said Henny Penny.

'I saw it with my own two eyes, I heard it with my own two ears, and a piece of it landed, plomp, on my own tail,' said Chicken Licken.

'I think I had better come with you, and together we can all warn the king,' said Goosey Loosey.

So they all set off in a busy little line, until they met Turkey Lurkey.

'Goodness gracious me,' said Turkey Lurkey. 'Goosey Loosey, Ducky Daddles, Cocky Locky, Henny Penny, and Chicken Licken! What a fine feathered sight on such a morning. Where are you all trotting off to?'

'Oh, you must help us, Turkey Lurkey. The sky is falling down, and we must go and warn the king.'

'But how do you know the sky is falling down?' said Turkey Lurkey.

'Ducky Daddles told me,' said Goosey Loosey.

'Cocky Locky told me,' said Ducky Daddles.

'Henny Penny told me,' said Cocky Locky.

'Chicken Licken told me,' said Henny Penny.

'I saw it with my own two eyes, and heard it with my own two ears, and a piece of it landed, plomp, on my own tail,' said Chicken Licken.

'I think I had better come with you. Yes, that's the best thing, then we can all warn the king together,' said Turkey Lurkey.

So off they all went, smallest in front, biggest at the back, until they met Mr Foxy Woxy.

'Mmmm, good morning,' said Mr Foxy Woxy. 'Well, well, if it isn't Turkey Lurkey, Goosey Loosey, Ducky Daddles, Cocky Locky, Henny Penny, and Chicken Licken. Where are you all going to on such a fine morning?'

'Oh, help, Mr Foxy Woxy. The sky is falling down, and we must go and warn the king!'

'But how do you know the sky is falling down?' asked Mr Foxy Woxy.

'Goosey Loosey told me,' said Turkey Lurkey.

'Ducky Daddles told me,' said Goosey Loosey.

'Cocky Locky told me,' said Ducky Daddles.

'Henny Penny told me,' said Cocky Locky.

'Chicken Licken told me,' said Henny Penny.

'I saw it with my own two eyes, and heard it with my own two ears, and a piece of it landed, plomp, on my own tail,' said Chicken Licken.

'Then we shall all run together as fast as we can to my little den, for safety, and then I will warn the king,' said Mr Foxy Woxy.

So all together they scurried on their busy little feet into the dark den of Mr Foxy Woxy. And so it was that the king was never warned that the sky was falling down.

Sing, Sing

Sing, sing,
    What shall I sing?
The cat's run away
    With the pudding string!
Do, do,
    What shall I do?
The cat's run away
    With the pudding too!

Dance to Your Daddy

Dance to your daddy,
  My little babby,
Dance to your daddy,
  My little lamb.

You shall have a fishy
  In a little dishy,
You shall have a fishy
  When the boat comes in.

You shall have an apple,
  You shall have a plum,
You shall have a rattle-basket
  When your daddy comes home.

Bobby Shaftoe

Bobby Shaftoe's gone to sea,
Silver buckles at his knee;
He'll come back and marry me,
    Bonny Bobby Shaftoe.

Dame Trot

Dame Trot and her cat
   Sat down for a chat;
The Dame sat on this side
   And puss sat on that.

Puss, says the Dame,
   Can you catch a rat,
Or a mouse in the dark?
   Purr, says the cat.

The Brave Old Duke of York

Oh, the brave old Duke of York,
He had ten thousand men;
He marched them up to the top of the hill,
And then he marched them down again.
And when they were up, they were up,
And when they were down, they were down,
And when they were only halfway up,
They were neither up nor down.

Clap Hands

Clap hands, Daddy comes
With his pocket full of plums,
 And a cake for Johnny.

The Old Woman in a Shoe

There was an old woman who lived in a shoe,
She had so many children she didn't know what to do;
She gave them some broth without any bread;
She whipped them all soundly and put them to bed.

75

Lazy Jack

Once upon a time, a long time ago, when the world was still full of marvels, there was a boy called Jack. He lived with his mother at the edge of a fine country town. They were very poor, and Jack's mother did as best she could, and worked very hard for their living. She knitted woollen socks for all the local gentry. She worked from dawn till dusk, wearing out her poor old fingers. Her son Jack, on the other hand, did nothing. During the hot summer months he would sit around in the garden, fanning himself.

Then he would hog the best of the fireplace during the long cold winters.

Everyone shook their heads and called him Lazy Jack. His mother did her best, but she could never persuade him to lift a finger to help. Finally, one day she said that, 'enough was enough'. He must go out and work to help pay his way, or she would turn him into the street, and no one would want to help Lazy Jack!

Now this worried Jack, and bright and early the next morning he set off for a nearby farm. There he was hired to help, and at the end of the day he was paid with a shiny new penny. Jack walked home slowly in the evening sun. He spun his penny up in the air and generally showed it off to everyone, for he had never earned a whole penny before.

When he was nearly home, Jack lost the penny. It dropped in the water as he crossed the stream. His mother shook her head. 'I knew you were lazy, Jack, now it turns out you're daft as well. You should have put that penny safely in your pocket.'

'I will remember next time,' sighed Jack.

So early the next morning Jack set out and was given a job helping with the cows. At the end of the day, Jack was paid with a handsome jug of creamy fresh milk. Jack remembered what had happened to his penny. So he put the jug of milk deep into his trouser pocket, and set off home. By the time he got there, he had spilled all the milk, and the jug was empty.

'Oh dear me, Jack,' said his mother, 'what will become of you? You should have carried that on your silly head.'

'I will remember next time,' said Jack.

The next morning Jack set off in good heart to another farm. He was given a day's work helping in the dairy. At the end of the day, Jack was paid with a great round of delicious cream cheese.

'Mother will be pleased,' thought Jack, and, remembering what had happened to the milk in his pocket, he popped the round of soft cheese on top of his head and set off in the warm evening sun to walk home.

By the time he got home the cheese had melted and spoiled. It had run into his hair, and all down his shirt in a great sticky mess.

'I don't know, Jack,' said his mother. 'What a waste. Your shirt's ruined, and as for your hair, I can't even look. You should have carried that fine cheese carefully in your hands.'

'Sorry, mother,' said Jack. 'I will remember next time.'

The next morning Jack set out at cock-crow and was given a day's work by the baker. Jack worked hard all day in the hot bakery, and the baker paid him with a fine ginger tom-cat. Now Jack remembered what had happened to the cream cheese, so he took the tom-cat and began to carry it home very carefully in his hands. But this was a fierce and proud cat, and it began to yowl, and wriggle, and scratch. So much so that Jack had to let it go.

When he got home his mother could scarcely believe it. 'My word Jack, but you are a nincompoop. You should have tied a string around the cat and pulled 'im along behind you.'

'Sorry, mother,' said Jack. 'I will remember next time.'

Early the following morning, Jack found work from the butcher, and at the end of the day the butcher paid Jack with a fine ham on the bone. Now his mother would be pleased, it was just the thing to serve with a boiled cabbage. Then Jack remembered what had happened to the cat, so he tied a piece of string to the ham and pulled it all the way home behind him, through all the mud, and mess, and muddle of the streets. By the time he got home, of course, there was barely a shank of bone left at the end of the string: the ham was ruined.

His mother finally lost her temper, and fetched him a clout on the head. 'You're as daft as a brush. Now we've just cabbage for our dinner. You should have carried it on your shoulder.'

'Ow,' said Jack. 'Sorry, mother. I will remember next time.'

The next day Jack was hired by a wealthy merchant, who lived in a fine house nearby. Now this merchant was a widower who had a beautiful daughter. The daughter was very sad; she had neither laughed nor spoken for many years. All that week she had seen Jack from her window as he went off to his various jobs. Every evening she had watched him come home again.

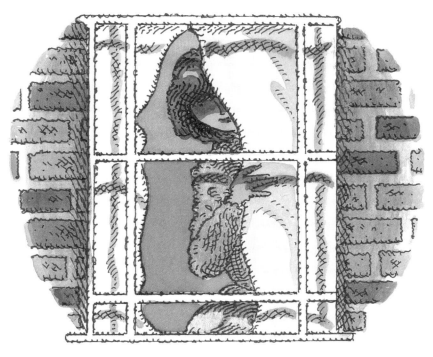

She had seen him lose his penny in the stream. She had seen him with milk spilling from his pocket. She had seen him with a great cream cheese melting into his hair. She had seen him struggling with a fierce tom-cat. She had seen him pulling a ham through the streets on a piece of string. Each time she had felt a little cheered up by the sight of Lazy Jack. (He was, after all, not a bad looking lad.) She could feel herself thawing inside like the river at the end of a long winter.

At the end of the day, the merchant rewarded Jack with a fine young donkey. Now Jack remembered what had happened to the ham, and with a great effort he swung the donkey up on to his shoulders. He began to stagger home with it. The merchant's daughter saw Jack from her window. He looked so silly trudging along with the donkey upside down across his shoulders and with its legs sticking up above his head, that she burst into great peals of golden laughter.

The merchant was so delighted to have his daughter restored to her old self that he sent for Jack and rewarded him with a gold sovereign. Jack straightaway put the sovereign in his pocket to keep it safe. Later in the year Jack married the merchant's beautiful daughter, and his mother was able to retire from knitting socks. She lived with them in their fine house, for the rest of her days, which was a very long time indeed.

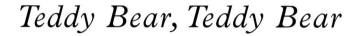

Teddy Bear, Teddy Bear

Teddy bear, teddy bear, touch the ground,
Teddy bear, teddy bear, turn right round,
Teddy bear, teddy bear, go upstairs,
Teddy bear, teddy bear, say your prayers,
Teddy bear, teddy bear, switch off the light,
Teddy bear, teddy bear, say Goodnight.

Rock-a-Bye, Baby

Rock-a-bye, baby,
    Thy cradle is green,
Father's a nobleman,
    Mother's a queen;
And Betty's a lady,
    And wears a gold ring;
And Johnny's a drummer,
    And drums for the king.

There Was an Old Woman

There was an old woman tossed up in a basket,
 Seventeen times as high as the moon;
Where she was going I couldn't but ask it,
 For in her hand she carried a broom.
 Old woman, old woman, old woman, quoth I,
 Where are you going to up so high?
 To brush the cobwebs off the sky!
 May I go with you? Aye, by-and-by.

Blow, Wind, Blow

Blow, wind, blow!
And go, mill, go!
That the miller may grind his corn;
That the baker may take it,
And into bread make it,
And bring us a loaf in the morn.

Down with the Lambs

Down with the lambs,
   Up with the lark,
Run to bed, children
   Before it gets dark.

Go to Bed, Tom

Go to bed, Tom,
Go to bed, Tom,
Tired or not, Tom,
Go to bed, Tom.

Index of Titles and First Lines of Poems

OXFORD
UNIVERSITY PRESS

Great Clarendon Street, Oxford OX2 6DP

Oxford University Press is a department of the University of Oxford.
It furthers the University's objective of excellence in research, scholarship,
and education by publishing worldwide in

Oxford New York

Athens Auckland Bangkok Bogotá Buenos Aires Calcutta
Cape Town Chennai Dar es Salaam Delhi Florence Hong Kong Istanbul
Karachi Kuala Lumpur Madrid Melbourne Mexico City Mumbai
Nairobi Paris São Paulo Singapore Taipei Tokyo Toronto Warsaw

with associated companies in Berlin Ibadan

Oxford is a registered trade mark of Oxford University Press
in the UK and in certain other countries

Text and illustrations copyright © Ian Beck 2000

The moral rights of the author/artist have been asserted

First published 2000

British Library Cataloguing in Publication Data available

ISBN 0 19 278164 2

Typeset by Mary Tudge Typesetting Services
Printed in Spain by Graficas Estella